To Dad
Dec - '88
from Roger + Darlene H.

CARTOONS

From the Newspaper Series "Memories of a Former Kid"

by **BOBARTLEY**

Iowa State University Press / Ames

To Ginny

Bob Artley began his career as an editorial cartoonist with the *Des Moines Tribune.* Most re-
cently he was an editorial cartoonist for the
Worthington (Minnesota) *Daily Globe.* Now re-
tired, Artley lives on the farm in Hampton, Iowa,
where he was born. Here he finds inspiration for
his writing and painting and still draws cartoons
for syndication by Extra Newspaper Features.

Originally published by Bob Artley © 1981
All rights reserved

Reprinted from the original without correction, 1989 by
Iowa State University Press, Ames, Iowa.

Manufactured in the United States of America

ISBN 0-8138-1068-X

Contents

Foreword

These drawings speak to us out of the universal province of memory.

Some of what we read strikes us as pretty but artificial; we enjoy it and forget it. Some of what we read strikes us as incredible or bizarre; these things we easily forget, too. Some of what we encounter in books or newspapers seems simply beyond judgment—irrelevant, or unremarkable, or outside our experience—and that we pass by.

But when the fully realized artist speaks to us, he speaks directly to our own memories. When we read such an artist, we remember thinking the same thought once, or experiencing once an identical moment, or having once just such an emotion. We are reminded by these shocks of recognition of what Joseph Conrad called the "solidarity of mankind." We are reminded of the tie that binds all humans together—the dead to the living, and the living to the unborn. This is why art is our great weapon against loneliness, which is the beginning of despair.

This may seem too much baggage to attach to Bob Artley's "cartoons," but it isn't. We may think we are charmed and moved by them because they are nostalgic, because they hark back to a quieter and lovelier time, because they are about Iowa, or about farm boys, or something. It is only incidentally so.

These drawings are, in fact, much better than that. At their core, they are not at all about long-ago farm life. They are about growing up, one of the half-dozen great themes of art, a theme Artley has addressed in a fresh and beautiful way. As his title suggests, he has discovered the child buried within himself, and he has dared to share that child truthfully with the rest of us. He reminds us of our own child-ness. He has put us into joyful touch with that forgotten part of ourselves.

For this, we are in Artley's immense and long-lasting debt.

PAUL GRUCHOW

3

CATTLE FEEDING HAS
ALWAYS HAD ITS
PROBLEMS — AS
WE REMEMBER

4

THE FIRST HONKERS
OF THE SEASON

7

8

9

13

14

15

16

17

18

19

20

21

22

23

24

25

26

27

28

29

LAST DAY OF SCHOOL

31

39

45

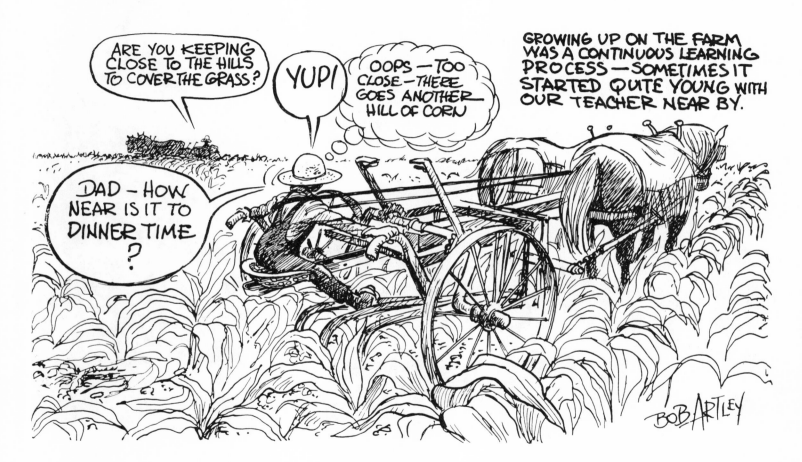

46

47

ON THE ONE-ROW CULTI-
VATOR I FELT LIKE A
SULKY DRIVER AT
THE COUNTY FAIR AS
I RACED (AND LOST) AGAINST
A SUDDEN SUMMER SHOWER

BOB ARTLEY

48

WHEN WE'D 'TAKE
A SHOWER' AFTER
A LONG, HOT
DRY SPELL

BOBARTLEY

49

51

53

THERE WERE TIMES WHEN THE SIMPLE TASK OF GOING ACROSS THE SLOUGH AFTER THE MILK COWS COULD BE COMPLICATED AND EXCITING

56

57

58

59

60

61

62

63

A CHEAP, SAFE WAY TO CELEBRATE THE FOURTH OF JULY WAS TO TURN THE IGNITION SWITCH OFF AND ON AS WE DROVE ALONG.

65

66

67

69

73

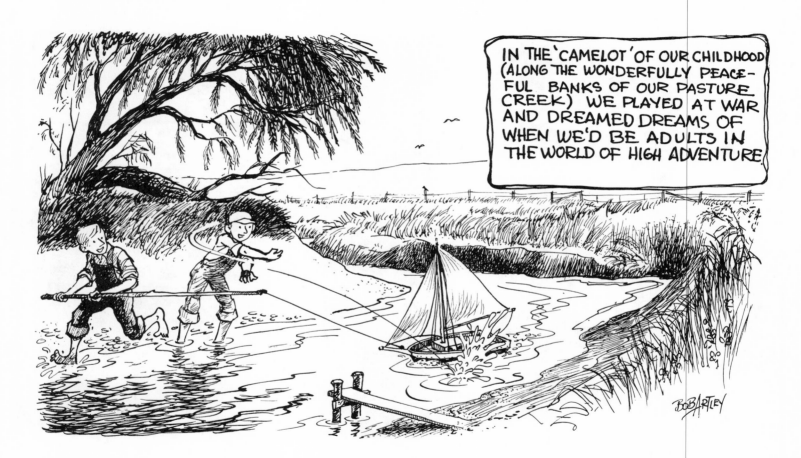

80

81

83

90

USUALLY, AFTER THRESHING TIME AND BEFORE SCHOOL STARTED IN THE FALL, WE'D TAKE ONE DAY VACATION TRIPS TO MASON CITY, WATERLOO, CLEAR LAKE OR SOME OTHER NEARBY PLACE OF INTEREST — OUR REST STOPS WERE AT COUNTRY SCHOOL HOUSES ALONG THE WAY

97

FIRST DAY
OF SCHOOL

BOB ARTLEY

98

101

WALKING HOME FROM SCHOOL WAS A DAILY ADVENTURE—ESPECIALLY OVER THE BRIDGE UNDER WHICH WE IMAGINED A TRAMP TO BE LAYING IN WAIT FOR US.

107

108

111

112

113

WE HAD CORN PICKING
VACATION IN COUNTRY SCHOOL
—AFTER A LONG, HARD DAY
IN THE CORNFIELD WE
COULD RELAX BY THE
SOFT LIGHT OF THE
KEROSENE LANTERN
IN THE
COWBARN

116

117

119

121

123

124

126

128

IT SEEMED LIKE GRANPA HAD AN AWFULLY LONG LIST OF THAT FOR WHICH HE WAS THANKFUL — WHILE THE FOOD WAS GETTING COLD AND I WAS DYING OF HUNGER

141

142

143

149

150

WHEN 'TWELVE DAYS OF CHRISTMAS' WASN'T VERY PROMISING

159

WHEN WE WERE RESCUED
BY DAD FROM OUR BLIZZARD-
ISOLATED SCHOOL —
NO RESCUE AT SEA COULD HAVE
BEEN MORE WELCOME

160

161

163

166

169

WHEN THE BIG KID
VISITOR TO OUR
NEIGHBORHOOD
SHOWED US AND
OUR SLEDS UP
WITH HIS NEW
"FLEXIBLE FLYER"

BOBARTLEY

170

171

172

174

175

176

179

182